This book belongs to

_____

WHAT AM I?

a collection of short stories

Color Edition

Color Edition
v. 3.1.0

All About® Learning Press, Inc.
615 Commerce Loop
Eagle River, WI 54521

ISBN 978-1-935197-75-1

Stories:
Marie Rippel:	"Twist and Stomp" – "The Grump"
	"The Bantam Spy Club" – "Open Rink"
	"The Bake Sale" – "Matt the Musk Ox"
	"Whale Songs" – "Champ" – "Pine Tree Pet Shop"
Renée LaTulippe:	"An Elf in the Swiss Alps" – "Broken Robot"
	"Skunk Hotel" – "Jake the Snake" – "What Am I?"

Illustrations:
Donna Goeddaeus:	"Twist and Stomp" – "The Grump"
	"The Bantam Spy Club" – "Open Rink"
	"The Bake Sale" – "Whale Songs"
	"Skunk Hotel" – "Champ" – "Pine Tree Pet Shop"
Dave LaTulippe:	"An Elf in the Swiss Alps" – "Broken Robot"
	"Matt the Musk Ox" – "Jake the Snake" – "What Am I?"

Contributors:	Samantha Johnson, Jon Stenschke, Rebecca Webber
Cover Design:	Dave LaTulippe
Page Layout:	Dave LaTulippe, Andy Panske
Colorization of Stories:	Donna Goeddaeus

What Am I?: a collection of short stories is part of the
All About® Reading program.

For more books in this series, go to www.AllAboutReading.com.

To the reader—

*between these covers
you will find
silliness and facts
of every kind ...*

especially for you

Contents

Twist and Stomp

"You can win this! Trust me—you are the best," said Fox.

11

"Stunt 1 will be the pigs," said Fox.

"Stunt 2 will be the dogs. And then you will be up next."

"You are up!" said Fox. "Swing with the song."

"Stomp with the drums."

"Slip and spin."

"Twist and flex."

"Hop up. This is the big end," said Fox.

The best stunt
will WIN!*

"Grasp his hand. Stand on top. You can win!"

"Or not!"

The End

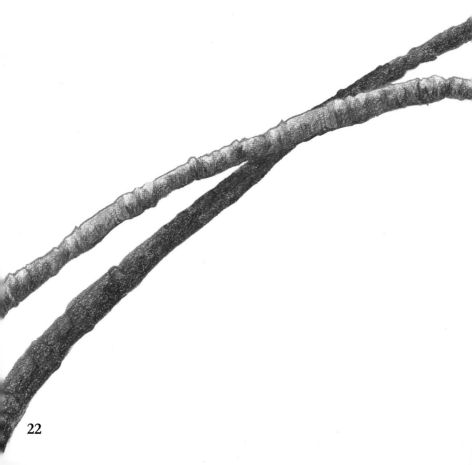

The Grump

I am not a shy lapdog.

I am not a fat frog.

I am not a sly muskrat.

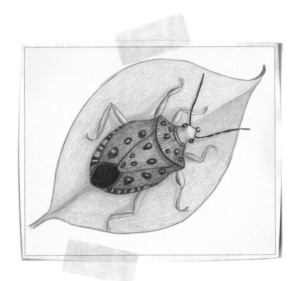

I am not a stinkbug.

I am just a grump.

I cannot quack or swim.

I cannot hiss or slink.

I cannot sting or fly.

I cannot stomp or cry.

I am just a grump.

I wish I had fast fins to swim.

I wish I had swift wings to fly.

I wish I had long legs to run.

I wish I had big quills to prick.

I am just a grump.

29

I will just sit on this branch.

I will just spin my silk.

I will just hang on this trunk.

I will just nap in my stiff, dry sack.

I am just a grump.

But ... GASP!

I can pry myself from my sack.

I can dry my wings in the sun.

I can dash and bend and swish.

I can flap and clap and twist.

I can fly!

I am NOT a grump!

The End

The Bantam Spy Club

I am Ellen and this is Dennis.

We are in the Bantam Spy Club.

We have a big problem.

The club mascot, the Bantam Chicken, is lost.

We are upset.

We think the Muskrat Club has him.

Can you help us?

Can you be a spy?

Can you run fast?

Can you be sly?

Can we trust you?

If you said "yes," grab this spy hat
and get set to go!

We intend to get the Bantam Chicken back.

We have a plan.

The plan is on this napkin.

Dennis will flap and cluck
and quack.

Sit still until Dennis quacks.

Then … run!

Go to the wigwam of the Muskrat Club.

Grab the Bantam Chicken.

Tuck him in your spy hat.

Then run back to us. Be quick!

Run as fast as you can!

Go! Run! Run!

You got the Bantam Chicken back
from the Muskrat Club!

You are the best spy!

This is a spy pin just for you!

The End

An Elf in the
Swiss Alps

This is me on my trip to the
Swiss Alps.

The Alps go up, up, up into the sky!

I have soft mittens, thick socks, and
a hat to block the strong wind.

I met Ed in the Swiss Alps.

Ed is an elf. He has a red hat
with a bell.

Ed is shy, but he is fun to be with.

Ed has a pet ostrich that he got
as a chick.

Oz the ostrich was just a bunch of
fuzz back then. She snacks on insects.
She got big fast!

Oz has big wings but cannot fly.

She runs fast with her long legs.
That ostrich is so quick!

Ed sits on her back as I sled by.

Ed tends his flock in the glen.

The flock is content to munch on grass.

Ed and I have a picnic on the bluff.

He invents a lunch with ham and nuts. Yuck!

Ed insists I try it. It is not bad!

Ed can do fun tricks.

He can twist and flip and
do the splits.

He can spring into a handstand.

I do a handstand next to Ed.

Ed tells me it is fun to jump
in the slush. I try it with him.

STOMP! SPLASH! It is a blast!

My socks get wet.

We stop at an inn to rest.

We drink a cup of eggnog with nutmeg.

Then we hang up the wet socks.
We sit with a snack as the socks dry.

I am sad that my trip must end.
I had a lot of fun, but I must go.

I will miss Ed, his ostrich, and his
flock. And I will miss the Swiss Alps!

The End

Open Rink

Chick and her pals sit next to the rink.

But big, bad Hog stops Rat.

Um ... can we go on the rink with you?

This will be a big event! Do you think Chick and her pals will win?

The ref drops the puck into the rink.

Chick has the puck. She hits it to Cat. Hog blocks the puck!

Hog sends the puck to Yak.

Get the puck, Yak!

Yak hits it to the end of the rink.

Rat protects the net. He will not let the puck get by!

Rat hits the puck to Chick.

Go, Chick! The puck is yours! Go for the net!

Yak grabs the puck from Chick ...
but he runs into Cat!

Chick gets the puck back.
She hits the puck with her stick …
… past Hog
… past Ram
… and into the net!

Chick is a hero!

Cat hits the puck to Yak.

The pals have fun!

The End

Broken Robot

Jan. 12, 2025

Zigzag Robot Shop
634 Robin St.
Red Wing, MN 55066

To the Zigzag Robot Shop:

Rob the Robot was a gift from my mom. She got him from your shop.

I regret to tell you that Rob is a bad robot. I must send him back for a refund.

Problems began the moment I got the box lid open. Rob sprang from the box and began to smash my trumpet. Stomp, stomp, stomp!

"No!" I said, but Rob did not stop until my trumpet was just a lump of brass.

"OK, we must discuss this," I said. But Rob fled and hid in the shrubs until dusk.

Rob is such a pest. He gulps my milk and shreds my napkin. I cannot even finish my lunch.

If I ask Rob to stop, he bumps into plants or digs in the trash. Then he acts sad.

When we went to a hotel, he slung the lamps into the bathtub. Then he hit his fists on the bed until the springs went POP!

He did not stop at that. Rob went on to smash the TV and a desk.

The hotel staff sent us a bill for the broken things.

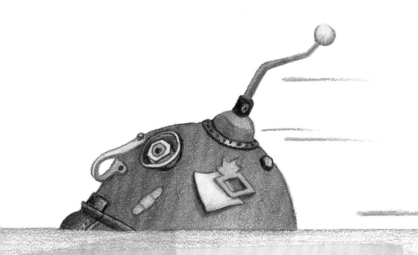

His helmet is a magnet, so stuff sticks to it. Rob will not let me get my things back!

He acts as if my stuff belongs to him.

And I must tell you the last thing.

If he gets mad, Rob yells insults and flings figs at my back.

As you can tell, Rob has a long list of bad habits. I must demand a refund!

Thank you,

Todd

P.S. Rob just got my pen. I am at my limit with him. Rob the Robot must go!

The End

The Bake Sale

Kate sat on the red bike at the bike shop. "I like this red bike! *My* bike has rust on it."

"Have a bake sale! Then you can get the bike," said Helen. "I can help you!"

"Yes!" said Kate. "Thanks!"

Helen and Kate ran home.

"Here is a cupcake mix," said Kate.
"Can you mix it up? Then we can bake
them."

Kate said, "I will set up a bake sale stand. We can set the sale items on top of this desk."

Helen set the milk next to the cupcake plate. "The bake sale is open!"

Sang came up to the stand. He gave Kate $1.00.

"I will have a cupcake and a glass of milk," said Sang.

"Thank you! I hope you like them," said Kate.

Sang ate a bite of the cupcake.

"Mmmm!" he said.

Dave and Nate came to the stand. "We will take a cupcake and milk," said Dave. He gave Kate $1.00.

More kids came to the stand. Helen said to Kate, "I think you will get that red bike!"

At the end of the sale, Jane came to the stand.

"Hi, Jane!" said Kate.

"Hi, Kate! I just got a note from my pen pal," said Jane.

"From Beth?" said Helen.

"Yes," said Jane. "Beth and her mom take care of sick dogs and help them get well. But she must have more cash for the rent."

"Can we help the sick dogs?" said Helen.

"I wish," said Jane.

"We *can* help the sick dogs!" said Kate. "We can send Beth the cash from the bake sale."

Helen said, "But you cannot get the red bike if you send the cash to Beth!"

Kate said, "That is OK. My bike is not so bad. It still runs fine and I can shine it up. I am glad to help the dogs."

Sang said, "We can have a bike fix-it shop! We can fix bikes and shine them up! Then we can send the cash to Beth to help the dogs."

Kate and Helen said "Yes!" at the same time.

The kids made lots of cash to help
the dogs!

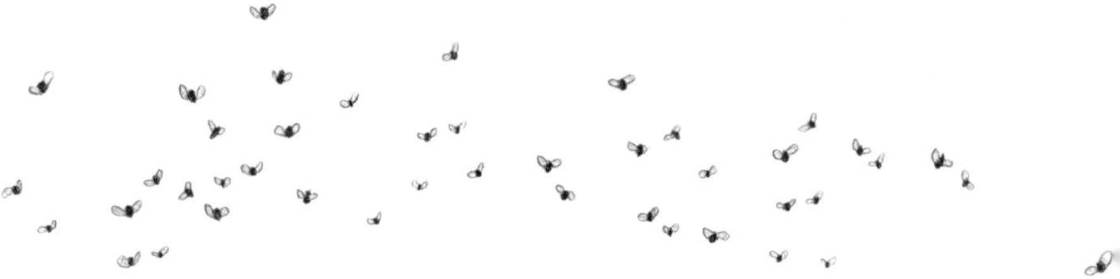

Matt the Musk Ox

It was June. Matt the musk ox went to the lake for a swim.

Deb the dog sat on a dune by the shore.

The musk ox said to Deb,
"Hi! My name is Matt. I came to take a swim."

Deb said, "Not to insult you, but musk oxen smell bad! This lake is for *dogs*, not for musk oxen. Oxen must use the silt ponds past the hill. That is the rule."

Matt was sad. He did not think he had a bad smell.

Matt began the long hike back to his home.

Deb the dog was smug. She did not have to share the lake.

Deb went for a swim. But she got stuck in quicksand!

Deb began to sink!

"Help!" said Deb with a yelp. "I am stuck in the muck! I will sink!"

The sudden cry made Matt
stop in his tracks.

He got a rope and ran back to
the shore.

Matt said, "Grab this and hang on!"

Matt gave a strong tug.

Deb rose from the muck and made
it back to the dune.

Deb was safe!

Deb said, "Thanks a lot! You are my hero!"

Matt said, "No problem. I am glad I was here to help."

Deb gave Matt a lick on his nose to thank him.

Deb said, "You can swim with me! The rule will be that the lake is open to dogs *and* musk oxen."

Matt said, "Do I still smell bad to you?"

Deb said, "A rose smells bad next to my pal, Matt the musk ox!"

Deb and Matt sat on the dune as the sun set.

Deb said, "I admit I was selfish and rude. I wish I was more like you!"

Matt said, "You can be! I think you are a fine dog."

Deb gave Matt a big hug as the sun sank in the sky.

The End

Whale Songs

Duke swam next to his mum.

"I am a *big* humpback whale!" he said.

"You *are* a humpback whale, but you are not big yet," said his mum. "You are still a kid."

Whack!

Duke made a big splash.

"I can still do something big!" said Duke.

That made Mum grin.

Just then, Tang the fish swam up.

"We have a problem! Whisk the white whale is stuck in a net! He cannot swim!"

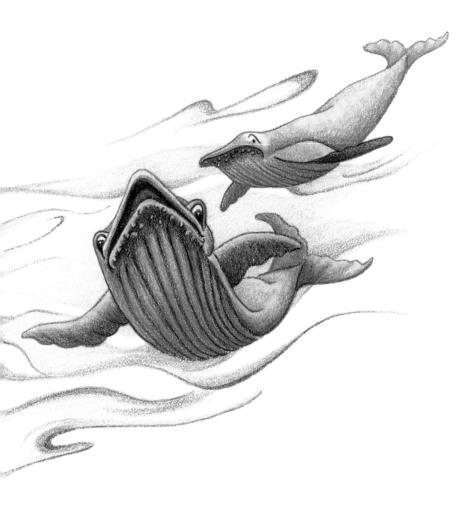

"That is bad!" said Duke.

"We must go help Whisk!" said Mum.

Duke, Mum, and Tang swam to Whisk.

"Whisk, we will help you! You can depend on us!" said Duke.

Whisk was glad to have some help.

"What can we do?" said Tang.

Duke said, "We can ask Wade the crab to help! He can cut the net open. If we sing a whale song, he will come as fast as he can."

"What is a whale song?" said Tang.

Duke said, "A whale song is like a long hum. Then we add clicks and grunts."

Duke and his mum began to sing the whale song.

Wade swam in. "What can I do for you?"

"Whisk is stuck in a net!" said Duke.

"I will cut the ropes!" said Wade.

Snip, snip, snip! Wade cut the net.
Whisk was safe!

Mum said to Duke,
"You did something big!"

Duke swam off with a splash.

The End

Skunk Hotel

It is spring, and it is time for the skunk to fix up a home for himself.

The skunk spots a crate in an open shed.

This broken crate will make a fine nest! The skunk begins his tasks.

He cuts twigs to size to make a bed frame. A pile of grass will finish the bed and protect it from damp drafts and frost.

The skunk can use these rocks to make a path to his home.

On top of the crate,
the skunk hangs rags with
a bit of twine and rope.

He is content with his safe home.
Time to doze for a while!

But then … what is this? A man
opens the shed! The skunk and the
man stare, frozen for a moment.

"Is this a skunk?" the man asks.
"It is black with a white stripe on
its back. Yes, it is a skunk in a crate!
But why?"

"You do not belong in here!
My shed is not a skunk hotel!"

"But you are so cute!" the man admits.
"Do not hide from me."

"I like you," the man tells the skunk.

"A lone skunk is not a problem.
You can use this shed for a home."

The skunk is glad that the man is
not upset.

But the man is not so wise …

for the next time he opens the shed,
the skunk will have five kits and a wife!

The End

Champ

Champ is a pony with a long mane and forelock. He has spots on his rump and a white blaze on his nose.

Champ's brushes sit on a shelf. His ropes hang on a peg and his blankets rest on a trunk.

Clare takes care of Champ.

Her list of chores hangs in the shed.

When Clare checks off the last item,
she and Champ can go for a ride.

Clare stands on a bench to get on Champ's back. He stands still while she gets on.

Clare rides Champ for miles.

Clare and Champ stop to rest by a lake. The pony dips his nose in the lake and takes a drink.

Clare wades in the lake. She spots a pile of sticks by the shore. Clare thinks that the hill is a den made by a muskrat.

Yes! It *is* home to a muskrat! Swish! The muskrat dives in.

Time for lunch. Clare sits in the grass with a sandwich and grapes.

A chipmunk comes close. Clare tempts him with a grape. He sniffs it.

Then, quick as a flash, the chipmunk grabs the grape and dashes off with it.

Clare is glad to spend time with Champ. She trusts Champ and Champ trusts her.

The pony munches on the grass. The grass has a fresh smell that Clare likes.

Insects buzz and frogs chime in. A robin adds his song.

Then it is silent.

Crash!

"Run like the wind, Champ!"

Clare pretends that Champ is a
fast mustang as he runs back to the
ranch. Drops begin to splash them.
Clare hangs on to Champ's neck and
smiles into the wet wind.

Champ is brave and gets them home safe. Clare hugs her pony.

"Thank you, Champ!"

The End

Pine Tree
Pet Shop

Miss Finch runs the Pine Tree Pet Shop on Reed Street. She broke her leg last week.

I have been at the store a lot to help her. I sweep, ring up sales, and help with odd jobs.

"I need to go home to rest my leg," said Miss Finch. "Can you run the store?"

"Yes, I will be glad to help!" I said.

Miss Finch pats me on the back. "Thanks. I am glad I can trust you."

Then Miss Finch has to go home. I get to run the store by myself!

"What jobs can I do?" I ask myself.

I check on the pet rats.

I give them boxes to nest in, and then I feed them.

A rat runs on the wheel while the rest of the rats sniff the seeds and boxes.

Quick as a wink, the rats dive into the boxes.

Why did the rats hide?

I freeze. I see what made them hide!

A green snake stares at the rats.

A snake—not in his tank!

I must get that snake back in his tank!

But I cannot. I cannot make myself pick up the snake and set it back in its tank. I do not like snakes.

But I must do it. Miss Finch trusts me to run the shop.

I peek into the tank. Not a snake is left! Seven snakes are free! I feel my skin creep.

A snake greets the rabbits.

A snake sleeps by the crickets.

A snake slides by the fish tanks.

And three snakes peer at the rats.

It scares me, but I grab the snakes
and set them back in the tank. I set
a big rock on the lid of the tank.

I like to take care of the pet shop,
but I do not like those snakes! I
think my next job will be to make
a strong lid from a sheet of steel.
Then those snakes cannot get free!

The End

Jake the Snake

Slip.
Slide.
Twist and glide.

I'm Jake the Snake.

I can hide in the shade of a rose.
I can pile up and pretend to be a hose.
I can smell and not even use my nose.

Can't you?

I can scrape my side on a broken rock.
I can shed my skin like a slung-off sock.
I can make kids gasp and stare in shock.

Can't you?

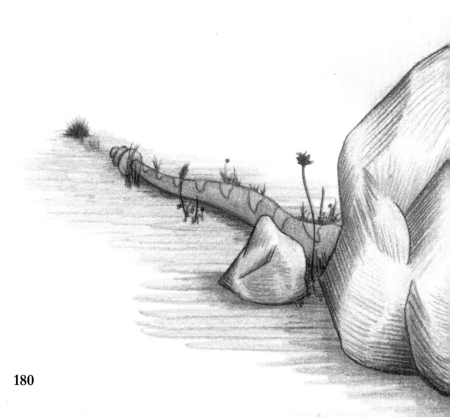

I'm quick and silent, swift and wise.
My stripes are cute and just my size.

My fangs protect me in the grass.
My scales shine in the sun like glass.

Slip.
Slide.
Twist and glide.

I'm Jake the Snake.

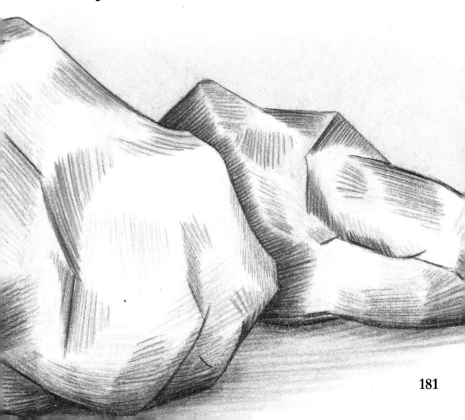

I can make my home in holes and caves.
I can slink and slide and swell like waves.
I can scare a brave man while he shaves.

Can't you?

I can twist my spine into lots of shapes.
I can gulp an egg or a bunch of grapes.
I can chase a cricket up the drapes.

Can't you?

Slip.
Slide.
Twist and glide.

I'm Jake the Snake.

I can hang from the branch of a tree.
I'm slick and strong. I'm fast and free.
I slink and swish—I'm glad I'm me!

I'm Jake the Snake.

Sssssssssssssssssss!

The End

186

What Am I?

Step on up
and don't be shy!
It's time for a game
of What Am I?

Test your skill!
(The hints are free!)
You'll see what fun
this game can be!

Hints:

I need a breeze and a long string to fly.

With your help, I go up in the sky.

Try not to get me stuck in a tree.

I hope you will run and fly with me!

What am I?

I am a kite!

I drift on the wind like a plane.

I zigzag and twist in the sky.

Hold on to my string!

If you said I am a kite,
then here is a prize for you!

Next hints:

I have no feet, but my hands move fine.

I have a three, a six, a seven, and a nine.

I tick and I tock to get you to sleep.

*Then I wake you up with a chime
or a beep.*

What am I?

I am a clock!

I help you rise at nine and dine at five.

I tap a tune as time ticks by.

Trust in me and you won't be late!

If you said I am a clock,
then here is a prize for you!

Next hints:

I can be black or red or even green.

I live inside a pen, unseen.

You can dip in me with a quill.

I make a big mess if I spill!

What am I?

I am ink!

With the help of your pen, I can tell
jokes that make you smile!

We can invent spy codes and
spin tales of brave deeds.

If you said I am ink,
then here is a prize for you!

Next hints:

I am hot! I snap and flick.

I melt wax and even plastic.

My flames can be red or gold.

If I get on you, you need to STOP, DROP, and ROLL!

What am I?

I am fire!

I can help with your chores.

I can dry your wet mittens or hats.

I can help you bake muffins or fry lots of fish.

203

If you said I am fire,
then here is a prize for you!

Next hints:

If you jump in me, you will get wet.

You can see me crash on the rocks, I bet.

You can ride on me, and I won't mind.

*I drop shells on the shore
for you to find.*

What am I?

I am a wave!

I splash on the shore and dig holes
in the sand.

I swim with the whales and the
fish.

I shine like gold when the sun sets
on me.

207

If you said I am a wave,
then here is a prize for you!

You did your best,
you gave it a try.
Did you like this game
of What Am I?

It's fun to do,
so make up a quiz,
and see if your chums
can tell what it is!

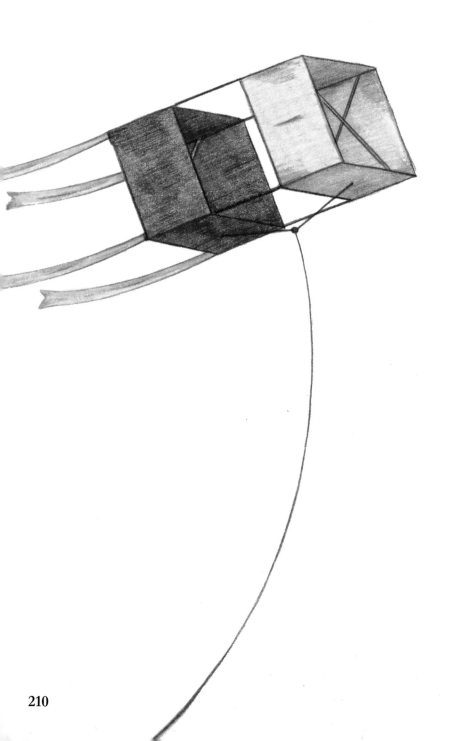

The End

You did it! You made it!
You got to *The End*!
But more fun is coming,
my book-reading friend!

So pull up a chair
or the branch of a tree.
You're ready for reading—
now open *Queen Bee*!